John Dugall

a great
gathering
today

in

Santa Fe

come again

Jerun
22 October
2020

Also by James McGrath from Sunstone Press

At the Edgelessness of Light, 2005
Speaking with Magpies, 2007
Dreaming Invisible Voices, 2009
Valentines and Forgeries, Mirrors and Dragons, 2012

The Sun is a Wandering Hunter

Poems
James McGrath

Drawings
Ottelie Loloma

SUNSTONE PRESS

SANTA FE

On the Cover: "Sequafnehma," wax and ink, by James McGrath. Award in Painting, Southwestern Artists Biennial, Museum of New Mexico, 1964. Photograph by Laura Gilpin.

The Sun is a Wandering Hunter is published with grants from Lore of the Land and the 2012 New Mexico Literary Arts Gratitude Award.

All Sun Clan Symbols in this book are from *Designs on Preshistoric Hopi Pottery* by Jessie Walter Fewkes, Bureau Of American Ethnology, Washington, Government Printing Office, 1919.

Sunstone books may be purchased for educational, business, or sales promotional use. For information please write: Special Markets Department, Sunstone Press, P.O. Box 2321, Santa Fe, New Mexico 87504-2321.

Body typeface › Trebuchet MS
Printed on acid-free paper
∞
eBook 978-1-61139-338-5

Library of Congress Cataloging-in-Publication Data
McGrath, James, 1928-
[Poems. Selections]
The sun is a wandering hunter : poems / by James McGrath ; drawings by Ottelie Loloma.
    pages ; cm
ISBN 978-1-63293-033-0 (softcover : acid-free paper)
I. Loloma, Otellie, 1922-1993 II. Title.
PS3613.C497A6 2015
811'.6--dc23
                    2014036242

WWW.SUNSTONEPRESS.COM
SUNSTONE PRESS / POST OFFICE BOX 2321 / SANTA FE, NM 87504-2321 /USA
(505) 988-4418 / ORDERS ONLY (800) 243-5644 / FAX (505) 988-1025

Dedication

*I*n memory of Otellie Loloma,
Hopi artist-teacher 1922-1993,
who created the spirited
artwork in this book
by sharing the journey.

Contents

Preface

*O*tellie Loloma was born in 1922 at Sipaulovi Village, Second Mesa, Arizona, into a Hopi family, a Hopi family whose roots reach back into the first world, a time without name or date.

Otellie met poet-artist James McGrath in 1962. During thirty-one years, the two of them shared teaching at the Institute of American Indian Arts in Santa Fe, New Mexico, shared poems, drawings, paintings, shared letters when absent, shared timeless days of song and dances, *niquivi* and *piki* on the Hopi reservation, shared the sprouting of beans, the harvesting of corns, and shared winters of story telling.

This collection is an intimate collaboration of artist and poet, connecting the inner visions of both: the deeply traditional Native American and the earth-centered sensitivity of an Irish-descendant poet.

These poems reflect the traditional bardic song-poems of the McGrath ancestors, 12th to 16th century bards (Ollamhs) of County Clare, Ireland, bards to the O'Briens of Thomond, These poems reflect, as well, the traditional day-long dance song-poems heard in the Pueblo and Hopi Indian villages of the Southwest United States. Like these traditional indigenous forms, these poems and drawings have the one constant, almost mystical feeling for nature and its connection to the poet and the artist.

The cultural differences between Otellie and James were balanced by spirited creative similarities in their lives that birthed this unique narrative: part mystery, part ageless hunting, part without contemporary meaning, and part sun. This collection praises the continuous search for revealing the inner spirit in the artists' work and the poets' work.

Together, Otellie Loloma and James McGrath achieved what is not found in books: the gathering of word and image to build a cairn in the desert on the journey of two individuals. They created beginnings and endings and left an opening in their winter story for you to enter.

This collection is a dance through time inviting the reader to step into a rhythm inscribed on the stones and in the dust of the Southwest United States. These are songs between two poets, two artists who danced alone and together in a silent but penetrating world, writing and drawing together. This is part of the lore of the land that is creating art. This is loving.

"Life is a pure flame, and we live
By an invisible Sun within us."
        —Sir Thomas Browne

"A hunter knows life is all around, abundant.
It's what is hunted."
        —Larry Littlebird, Santo Domingo-Laguna, *Hunting Sacred*, Western Edge Press, 2001.

Introduction

*I*t is a late July afternoon and the Cloud People are coming. Some stand tall and solemn, silently rising higher and higher into the blue. Others lie heavy with dark bottoms. All are prelude to the lightning and thunderous cracks and sounds which will terrorize my dog, Crates, and will have my intense attention as I wait for the drops of water from the sky.

> I am asking for the rain.
> It is coming.
> It is here.
> It has left.
> Thank you.
> —James McGrath, 2009

The coming of rain is the climactic event of Pueblo life. Cloud People, lightning and thunder enliven our songs, dances and thoughts from dawn to dusk. Pottery, clothing and wall designs repeatedly depict this event. Each day is about remembering that rain and its drama assure our healthy survival in this place. The first rays of sunlight are gifted with cornmeal and the last glimmer of the setting sun is honored with words of thankfulness. While the sun is honored, the clouds are cherished. Here, at Santa Clara Pueblo, our world is framed by the Sangre de Cristos on the east and the Jemez Mountains on the west. Our Cloud People come, mostly off the Jemez. They darken our southwest sky and descend through the Santa Clara Canyon. First in stillness and then in sound, they bless us and move across the river and the valley. We are left astounded. The cycle of life is reaffirmed with each coming and going.

Pueblo people are about seeking life. To seek life is to know that we flow, we live within that life cycle. That we are one. We desire and pray:

> to complete the circle
> within you
> beyond you
> surrounding you.

These are words of James McGrath an Irish descendant poet and artist. Although McGrath has roots far away across the ocean, his earth-centered sensitivity easily connects with the roots of the native southwest people. I first met James many years ago in Hopi during a visit to their reservation school for some government agency. He was an art teacher living in a trailer next to the school. Typical to his character, he responded to a young timid Pueblo woman by inviting me to lunch. I was magnetized by this Anglo person who lived gracefully in an assigned mobile home on the Hopi reservation. I would guess that it was during his time there that he began to realize his "spirited creative similarities" with the Pueblos, Hopis—and with Otellie Loloma. That journey and the intertwining of inner visions is beautifully, respectfully and lovingly shared in this collection of poems.

> One day
>> I shall be a cloud
>> and I shall bring you the storm
>> who is energy
>>> and song
>>> and dance
>>> and growth
>>> and creativity.
>
> I shall cross the sky
>> and I shall cross the earth
>> I shall pause with you.

I shall sing and dance and grow forever
and in that myth
I shall return
again and again
to earth
to myself

and continue in the myth

that is the gray fox
that is the yellow fox
and that is the sun
and that is love.
—James McGrath, 1973

I met Otellie Loloma some years after she and McGrath had begun teaching at the Institute of American Indian Arts in Santa Fe. When I visited her studio on the Institute campus, she was completely engrossed in creating a clay figure. A group of students watched. Her hands were familiar. They were like the hands of my relatives at Santa Clara Pueblo. She moved unselfconsciously and confidently. She knew clay, Clay-Old-Woman, who responded to her fingers with kind acknowledgment. Communication between them was easy.

I smile at her drawings in this work which circle around McGrath's words of the spiritual adventurer who is both the hunter and hunted. In soft words he expresses becoming this, that and the other. The adventure, he claims along with the Pueblo people, is to experience the cycle of nature from within and without and to know that we are the drama. McGrath expresses the spiritual adventure as gently as he lives. His seeking, searching and finding relationship in the silences, sounds and textures of the journey encourage us "to enter dawn and become a new day" together.

—Rina Swentzell, Santa Clara Pueblo, New Mexico, Author of *Younger-Older Ones Tieu-Paadeh Ing*, 2010, The Canelo Project. Architectural Designer, Artist, Aural Historian.

15 ✳

The Day begins and ends
with the softness
of beans sliding
from one woven grass basket
edged in cloud designs
into another.

Concentrate on the sliding of the beans
softly in the morning
softly in the night.

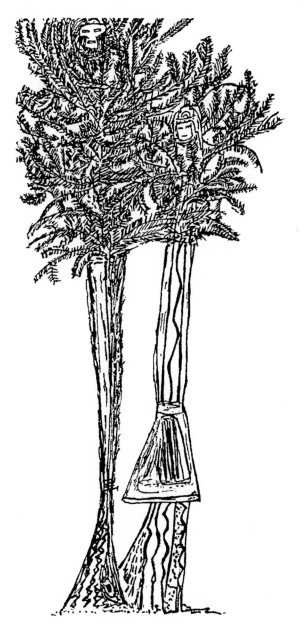

Before looking at the sun

> a hunter places a coating of corn pollen in
>
> his mouth
>
> on his tongue
>
> sweet corn pollen
>
> the sweetness that is there before the
>
> bee finds it.
>
> Then as the goldness of pollen
>
> fills the mouth
>
> cleans the mouth
>
> a hunter lifts his eyes
>
> up to the rising sun
>
> speaks to the morning sun
>
> and gathers the sweetness within himself.

On the first morning

> the sun was high behind the East cliff
>
> and it soon began to crawl down the
>
> West cliff
>
> and the eyes followed its wave
>
> > upon wave
> >
> > upon wave
> >
> > and it moved down the tree tops
> >
> > along the talus cones
> >
> > between the grass clumps

over the lichened stones revealing the earth
becoming the earth.

The song came from inside
somewhere
sweetness again
and became the wind
the wind became the song
the grasses danced more in
rhythm
the trees moved next in rhythm
the earth spun gold
spun sweetness
spun green
spun oneness
spun a great web
catching a hunter
lifting the feet of a hunter up
along a trail
down the tree tops
along the talus cones
between the grass clumps
over the lichened stones
revealing the earth
becoming the earth.

On the night before
the winds
were silent dancers
moving along the pines
and the spruce
and dropping bits of green
marking trails
in the broken branches
across blankets of pine
needles
rhythmically
marking trails
for a hunter
to follow
and the green bits of the dancers' trails lead into
forest places alive with
the rabbit light
turned to deer light
and a hunter can feel
the hoof of the deer
leave the ground
all around
to melt into the
pine trees
the movements to become the
breath of the wind

the color to become the
　　gray and ochre of the pine and spruce
the smells to become the
　　sweetness of
　　the red paintbrush
　　the yellow primrose
　　the blue larkspur.

And all
　　all seeps under
　　the spirit of a hunter
　　and the light
　　　envelopes
　　　and shrieks off the
　　　pine needles
　　　　　piercing
　　　making the bullets
　　　　　arrows
　　　making the gun
　　　　　a bow of rainbow
　　　making a hunter
　　　　　naked like
　　　　　mountain stone
　　　　　naked like a
　　　gray twisted cedar stump
　　　and the rattle of the
　　　words permeate a hunter

setting up sound waves

that weave in and out

of the body

in and out of the stones

in and out of the grass clumps

up the trees

jumping to the clouds that chase after

the deer shadows

and all this pulse

  all weaving

  waving in and

  out of the hunter.

And when it is time

the time for a hunter

to be hunted

the deer comes

bringing the light.

The light comes like a great

stream from the brown

dark eyes of the deer

piercing

a hunter

naked like the dancer

who passed that way

last night

dropping bits of his
greens
leading a hunter on to
find himself.

The light passes through
a hunter
passes through the light
and in the pause between the
dance
a hunter rests centered in clumps of
grass
bouncing
weaving
in the air currents left by
the deer.
And the grasses move
rhythmically
and a mound of
early blooming lupine
now in seed pods
shakes near the ears
of a resting hunter
connecting a hunter. This is the arrow
of the deer.
The bow is the deer's body.

And the deer comes.
The pollen sweetness
draws him.

The song from a hunter carried
by the wind leaping from
grass clump to lichened stone
to tree top to seed pod
to deer brought the deer to a hunter. This
is their connection.

The deer comes.
The hunter is hunted.
The sun swallows them
in the sweetness,
and the earth

    the grass clumps

    the tree tops

    the insects

    the seed pots

    all stop!

Stop, in the sweetness of the second

    of a hunter and a deer

    meeting.
And the morning corn pollen
is sweeter
the wind song is clearer
the sun is warmer
and the earth is covered again by
the green path of the dancer
as a hunter and a deer
move home!

The Night begins and ends
with the sprouting
of songs flowing from
one trail to the heart
edged in spruce boughs
to another.

Concentrate on the flowing of the songs
softly in the night
softly in the morning.

Dance of the Animals

The sun rose

over there 14 times

14 times it rose

as buds of fire bloomed

first there

then there

and as one bud

     and another

     died

     disappeared

others rose and bloomed

spotting the night hillside

in 14 times 14

buds

on the hillside.

Hunters moved

against the flaming flowers

moved in darkened

     rhythms

and began to gather

as their pulses

     together

as their bodies
and their spirits hunted for themselves
among the green cedars.

Sooner

the sun rose one times one singly
the sun rose
over there
glowing along the ground
sliding down the hillside
touching those with chilled feet and
anxious eyes
who waited and watched
below
touching them in the glowing beat
of itself
as the sound pulse entered
and enveloped their ears
rifle cracks
ripped the earth open
letting out the deer and the elk
letting out the antelope and the buffalo
and letting out all forms of
spiritual beings who entered
and enveloped

        the earth
        the sky
        those who waited and watched below
        and all those who hunted the
                hillside and carried the animals
                along the spirit paths into the
                village plaza.

The hillside
        beat
the hillside received the sun light
        beat
the hunters
swarmed
about the animals' pulse beat
from all sides
from the fires
now coals
from secret night places
from the dark night beat
the hunters
gathered to lead the animals
to the village
from the hillside
down over trails

tapped firm by past hooves and hunters' feet
down over sun-tipped grassy clumps
down the trails
   picked clean by winter mice
   down the trails
   across tracks of quail and fox
   joining tracks of quail and fox
into the gardens
   the corrals
   the back yards of the village people
toward the lines
of blanketed women and children
   from the village
who have wrapped their striped
   and diamond blanket of silence
   and strength about themselves
   silence and strength
   silence and strength
   beating
   beating
   reds
   blues
   ochres
   greens

stripes of silence
diamonds of strength
pulsing
pulsing
growing out of earth
at the edge of the village
people
waiting to receive the animals
and the hunters
to bless them with corn meal.

All silence
All strength
All beauty
All peace
in the village plaza
the hunters become a song
a song of blankets and bells
and waving spruce boughs
and clouds called feathers
and at once all men
become a single song, a single voice
to say thank you for coming
thank you for being here
dance for us
bring good life for us,

Thank you.
Thank you.
The song becomes all man
   the song is Mother Earth and Father Sky.
All is here
over here in the dancing foot
over here in the singing heart
over here in the listening ear.

And the day is filled again and again
         with sky again and again
with earth again and again
and in between are rainbow people
changing from rain to plant to cornmeal
         to pollen again and again
and all in between are love embers
         to heat and to begin flames
         for the rain to soften
         again and again.

And in the days that follow
         the many days that follow
         the sun rises over there
         the sun sets over there

and then

together

all men together

    find the time

    the moment

the clouds breath

to look up for the rain to soften us

    to make us the plant

      the cornmeal

      the pollen

then we shall sing and dance together forever.

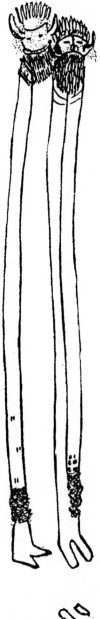

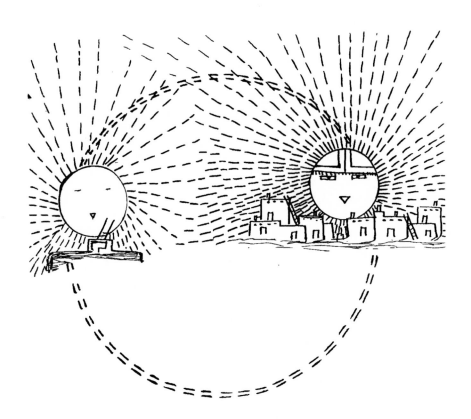

Moving
not alone
in silence
it will come again
be still
in silence
it never left
be still
in silence
you are silence
in silence
in silence
in silence.

It was beginning winter
It was mid-winter
and no winter at all.
All was in each embrace
untouching in the straightness and sureness
touching in the weaving of the roots.

Outside the adobe ovens
the Gods wafted
bits of winter at us behind
the windows—inside—
like beckoning us to come out to be
out

then standing
in the chilled fire-pit of the day
anticipating something beyond ourselves
something of our inside
too close
too soon

the voices of the bell
the feet
the rattle
the spruce branch
the caressing of wool against wool
of blankets
all voices
each a voice.

We were opened like milkweed pods
fingered against an imagined
          sun like a quartz pebble
plucked and incised
          and whittled at as a willow branch
          flute is carved and tested
and nibbled at by the baby teeth
          of the early morning
               early morning wind
from the East hills and the West
river that we could not see
because our eyes were nowhere,
our ears had taken them over!

And
so standing bits of the village roof,
we ushered in the new world
out of the old world
the always would be world.

And the world rushed us
broken bits that we were
under its blanket
          not for warmth
          not for protection
          but for love

and we became a turquoise thread
    a coral thread
    a chamisa gold thread
    a shell white thread
    a chokeberry violet thread
first one
then another
and then a snowflake came
    to our cheek
freezing into a star

snow bits turned shoulders and
    heads into the drifts of the day
like clouds settling on each of us
    to watch and to wait
    and so become.

The rhythms of the moment
matched the falling of the snow
and the sudden turns of the wind.
It was a part of the weaving process:
    winding
    knotting
    throwing
    beating

the yarn becoming a single line
then a double line multiplied into
a great pattern
finally the singleness
     the doubleness
     the multiplicity disappears
all meeting
and folding into the
     meaning of earth and man
     the Gods
       like you
       like me
     and the pattern?
     What of the pattern created?
     How could it be there in
       its flowering when the
       wind was rising
       and the snow kept pushing
       the colors
into the earth like the rains
     continually
falling on an uprooted field
unresisting
joyfully beaten down
folded under.
It was a he-rain action.

The blanket blobs of hot
summers and heated
autumn remnants received
the beatings as a tenderness
swelling in whiteness,
into the nothingness, into time.
All like the folding-in of
the winds in a germinating
wheat field. A she thing.

As soon as the ears gave up
the hold on the eyes, all
senses recorded time
the journey of the spirit under
the snow into the ground pulsing
      pulsing
      pulsing
as the spring
brake fern and wild celery shoots
pulse to reach the sun
as the bird picks its shell husk
seeking life
each knowing it is needed to complete
      the circle
        within you
        beyond you
        surrounding you

so there was closeness this winter's
day that happens every day
        and the earth becomes more
packed
        more heavily imprinted with
prints of feet and more than feet
and in the openings between the toes
grows the snow
and falls the cornmeal
the vibrations of bouncing feathers
and bell heart
and the already caressings
of wool against wool.
All remains there.

The yarn foundation of the children
        in the front
hand-spun from the finger voices
of the men and growing-into-men
behind

warmed by the wall of these
voices, assured that the wall
was there for more than protection
more than support

but for them to climb upon
as little ones to find niches
in it here and there
to set their roots into
find nourishment
seek a resting place
to become
to face the sun and to give and to be
        taught.

The wall
the foundation
        was all movement.

Those niches between the mud house blocks
        caught the snow
        letting it filter as quickly
        as quietly as the sun filters
        and the wind filters.

It was all falling behind the eyes
        in and through the ears
        permitting the fingers
the spirit fingers
to make holes in the snow covering
to receive a sweet breath of earth
        brown corn

the tongue would rob a salty snowflake

that was caught within its

reach

and the early morning Western

        fog white light reflected the

        earlier morning Eastern

        fog white light.

Soon all around

over shoulders and roofs

and there where the scented

smoke broke its path

soon all was as the early East

        white

        whiter

        whiter

        whiter

        wind gusts intoxicated themselves

in the drive at the blankets

in the scurry of covering the visible

        world with its snow love.

As the eyes were filled more and more

        in whiteness

        all bleached bone and flower petal

and water and roots of feather
whiteness
more of the pulse beats could be absorbed.

The feet were not in a dance
but in the pulse
and the skin moved not in a dance
but in the pulse
the hair was crushed not in the
        snow lying upon it
but in the pulse
the eyes met the loved figure
        next to you, not in the acknowledging
of something shared
        but in the pulse
the blanket was pulled up more tightly
        not in the tightening
        but in the pulse.

All was the sun
All was the strength
All was the purity
All was the light
All was the pulse
All was the breath

But it was not all, this.
How could it be?

The deer pranced in even stick
    footfalls
the antelopes shook themselves free
    of their awareness
    and caution
    joined the
    widening all
entering each one there
replacing stale things
dead things.

The maiden
    the radiant maiden
    the maiden the snow flurries
could not reach
    all corn tears
    feather touches
    spruce greenness
seeded herself everywhere.

Her hands took the messages
    shook them
        not to mix
    but to single out.

She gave these to those who would
      receive them. The snow flakes
      were made purer and the
      people in the adobe and stone houses knew.

      And the buffalo ones
      the more than dancing
      granite-walled ones.

Their forces surrounded, invaded,
      searched out secret places
      to be received and were received
      gently
      fiercely
were given a place to hide from
      heart-sore hunters
were given a place to graze in
meadows of honey-stained grass
       spirits
and still they danced
and still it snowed
and still the earth trembled
and still it dances

and still it snows

and still it trembles

        it will never stop.

I danced it all

        I—the wind

        I—the tear

        I—the sunbeam

        I—the snow

        I—the pulse

        I—the breath.

The Sun
is a
Wandering Hunter

A time ago

the eye curve

of a new moon and I met in a single

      stream of autumn light

and we crossed the sky

with you at our side

with you at our side

we crossed the sky

the moon

you and I.

The rabbits joined

us early

in the rabbit light,

     our trip was warmed!

In the center of the night

      the fox joined us.

   In the fox light

   our trip was quickened.

   In the time after

    the fox meeting

the cry of the coyote

    joined us breathing

     and it speeded our pulse toward dawn.

Just before dawn

       the birds joined us: the moon,

the rabbit, the fox, the coyote cry, you

and I together,

we entered dawn

and became a new day.

Originally published in *Dance with Indian Children,* 1972, and as "Just Before Dawn" in *At the Edgelessness of Light,* James McGrath, Sunstone Press, 2005.

Loma Talungva

(Beautiful Morning in Hopi Man's Language)

This morning

    the mountain is humming

    stones held in its heart,

    trees, the chorus that sighs,

    clouds, the dancers with thunder,

    deer, the eyes,

    birds, the ears.

All these wait for the sun

    to call them at dawn

    to sing.

23 July 2011
Hotevilla, Hopi Reservation, Arizona

69 ✳

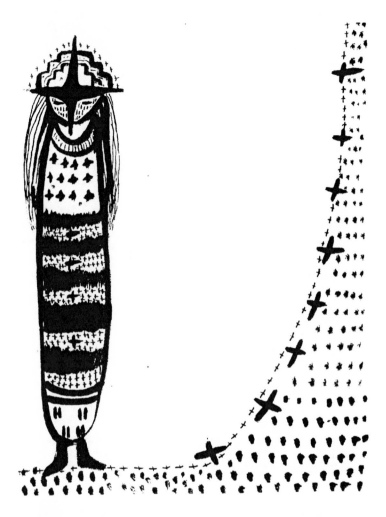

 Poems for the 5th World

After a Night of Wind

After a night of wind from the moon,
      I follow the dawn tracks of animals
      crossing the road.

I make human footprints
      that raise dust
tempting beetles
      to lose their way.

The silence under a July cedar tree
      holds tight to shadows.

Nothing moves except the anguish
      of an ant caught
      in the sweet honey of tree sap.

Yesterday a brown stone lay burnishing
      in the dust. This morning it was gone,
      encased in sand that had danced
      all night making drum beats
      with its family of smallest stones.

This is the land where spirit lives.

The body will wither,
      shake like dried corn stalks.

The spirit remains touched by clouds
      waiting to sing,
      waiting to be heard.

16 July 2006
Hotevilla, Hopi Reservation, Arizona

Silence

There is silence here
    when the moon speaks light.

Clouds become mountains,
    celebrate trees,
    praise melting snow,
    carve their images into stone and water.

Silence presses into the song
    of my hand,
    making a gift for time lost.

Silence moves the fingers
    into the clay and silver of the day,
    puts wings on the shadows that follow me.

19 July 2006
Hotevilla, Hopi Reservation, Arizona

My Dream Song

I will know my name
      when I come home.

It is my dream song.

This is where I stand
      when the sun rises.

It is my dream song.

20 July 2010
Hotevilla, Hopi Reservation, Arizona

They Say My Name is Corn

They say my name is corn.

They say I walked for centuries
        searching for home.

They say my path from the South
        gave me red,
        Paalangpu.*

They say my path from the West
        gave me yellow,
        Sekyangpu.*

They say my path from the North
        gave me blue,
        Sakwa.*

They say my path from the East
        gave me white,
        Qotsa.*

They say your land
        gave me life.

They say your song
        gave me life.

They say your dance
        gave me life.

They say your prayer
        gave me life.

They say I grow strong in soil called home.
        My name is corn.
        My name is home.

27 July 2011
Hotevilla, Hopi Reservation, Arizona

* Color words in the Hopi language.

 76

Over Here, Over There

Where does the horizon begin?
I must turn my head to find it.

    To the East clouds are resting.
    To the South clouds are resting.
    To the West clouds are resting.
    To the North clouds are resting.
    Here where I am sitting
      I am resting.

Where does the horizon end?
I must turn my head to find it.

22 July 2009
Hotevilla, Hopi Reservation, Arizona

This is My Art

I keep clouds in my eyes.

I keep images in my hands.

I weave myself into a basket
        to carry bread to my family.

This is my art.

You are my family.

I am a rattle in the earth.

When I sing birds listen to my song.

All about me are colors waiting
        for my heart and hands to dance.

There is a clown inside me.

It teases the rain from my eyes.

July 2010
Hotevilla, Hopi Reservation, Arizona

This is How I Walk

There are footprints in the sand
    that dance when the wind sings.

    This is how I walk.

There are trails between stones on the mesa
    left by foxes and coyotes.

    This is how I walk.

There are tracks on the branches
    of peach and juniper
    left by jays and bluebirds.

    This is how I walk.

There are pathways from yesterday to tomorrow
    left by ancestors.

    This is how I walk.
    This is how I walk home.

15 July 2008
Hotevilla, Hopi Reservation, Arizona

This is What My Uncle Said

Uncle said
Come walk with me.
We shall keep our eyes
on the earth.
Our eyes will become juniper berries.

Uncle said
We shall walk
as slowly as the turtle
as fast as the humming bird.
Our ears will become clouds.

Uncle said
Let us taste the water.
We shall have the tongues of fish.
Our mouths will become frogs.

Uncle said
Let us sit on a warm stone.
We shall smell flowers
while they are growing.
We shall breathe
      the red prayers of paintbrush
      the white prayers of rock roses.
Our bodies will become the color of tobacco.

My uncle said
      When we come home
      we will know our names.

14 July 2008
Hotevilla, Hopi Reservation, Arizona

House of Blessings

—For Robert Rhodes and Verma Nequatewa, Hotevilla

In the morning
    when the gray fox, the yellow fox,
    the red fox have run from the sky
    to the East, I walk the path
    to the House of Blessings.

The Path through *Munsi Tsomo* is edged
    in *Sohu*, the rock rose, *Munsi*,
    the paintbrush, *Ygapi*, the juniper.

My footsteps are brothers to the night dog,
    the morning lizard and the shadows
    of speechless trees.

The *Paalangpu*, red, of *Munsi*, warms my walk.

The *Qotsa*, white of the rock rose, gives me
the white light of morning.

I can not count the thousand and thousand footsteps
    rain left in the dust last night.

Somewhere in the *Hootski* a mocking bird announces
    songs to the clouds and sleeping stones.

The path will remember me by the footsteps
    I have left in the sand on my way to
    the House of Blessings.

This is how I walk when the sun rises
    and the gray fox, the yellow fox,
    the red fox and I go home each morning.

20 July 2011
Hotevilla, Hopi Reservation, Arizona

There is a Vein of Turquoise

There is a vein of turquoise
    from the home of my *Mö'wi*,*
    my family, to where I live.

When I stop along the path
    to think of them,
    rings hang from my ears
    to catch the poetry of Summer rain.

Drop by drop, my ears are inlaid
    with the song of dancing rain.

22 July 2006
Hotevilla, Hopi Reservation, Arizona

Mö'wi: a female in-law

Previously published in *Visions of Sonwai Verma Nequatewa* by Annie Osburn, Sonwai Inc., Hotevilla, Arizona, 2007

Vision Quest

Four nights now
      we have walked into the darkness
      toward the moon
      only to find ourselves
      shining back.

Four nights now
      we have walked above the earth
      where it is light
      and moon covered
      except for the deep tree shadows
      that are always present.

Four nights now we have been touched by the moon
      branded by its white fever
      melted in its palm.

Four nights now
      we have traveled toward home.

Previously published in *Dakotah Territory #6*, Winter 1973-74.

Rain in Five Parts

I am asking for the rain.

It is coming.

It is here.

It has left.

Thank you.

20 July 2009
Hotevilla, Hopi Reservation, Arizona

I Create with a Song

Like the stones on the mesa,
    like the night blooming datura along the road,
    like turquoise and corals I wear
    know where they belong.

They sing to me, "This is where I belong."

Like the kernels in the corn,
    like the melons in the field,
    the stones and woods I wear
    tell me their stories.

They sing to me, "This is where I belong."

In my heart's eye,
    my fingers dance the song
    of the ancient Hopi artists
    who inlaid turquoise on squares of wood.

I know where I belong.

12 April 2007
Santa Fe, New Mexico

In Rick's Field

I walked among corn
>dancing green this morning
>in Rick's field.

My first steps heavy
>leaving prints in the sand.

I walked among melons and gourds
>stretching their green arms this morning
>in Rick's field.

My ears listened for hints
>of rattle songs to come.

I walked among beans
>rustling their green leaves and tendrils
>this morning in Rick's field.

My tongue tasting
>the soft browning of future stews.

My eyes painted
>green corn tassels preparing
>for butterflies to dance
>among them.

My eyes painted
>a black beetle moving
>among corn, beans, gourds and melons
>humming its green song
>of beautiful mornings
>in Rick's field.

Stepping lightly
>leaving no footprints
>carrying growing green happiness
>that calms how I walk about the earth
>I left Rick's field.

17 July 2014
Hotevilla, Hopi Reservation, Arizona

One Long Poem

It is the repeating of silent rhythms
    that is dance and song
    the poem in this place.

It is the vision of earth colors
    red, orange, yellow, brown
    that is the poem in this place.

It is the small leaves of rock rose
    stipple pattern of cactus
    red tips of paintbrush, *munsi,*
    that is the poem in this place.

It is the open spaces between summer clouds
    breathing of summer winds
    rustle of junipers, *ygapi,*
    that is the poem in this place.

It is the morning sun blessing
    wren song, mocking birds, doves
    that is the poem in this place.

It is the unseen architect building sand hills
    leaving space for fields to green
    that is the poem in this place.

It is the open land that invites you
    into its place fullness
    that welcomes you here,
    that makes you the poem in this place.

It is when you become the poem
    in this place that you know
    you are home.

27 July 2014
Hotevilla, Hopi Reservation, Arizona

A Song for Otellie

Her hands were clay.

With clay fingers
 she made portraits of her *mö'wi,*
 her relatives.

With clay fingers,
 she made bowls for her *piki,*
 her blue corn bread.

I think of her pots,
 of the fullness inside
 where the treasures are held,
 secure and loved in their silence.

She gave me her secret—
her Hopi name, *Sequafnehma*—
the place in the valley where the squash
 blossoms bloom.

With her clay fingers,
 she gave me the bowl for the bear.

In the valley of my eye
 I see her now.
 her pollen covered face
 in the chamisa by the roadside
 in the last sunflower in my garsden.

With her clays,
 she lies under stones
 near Corn Rock
 and dances
 even now in winter
 with the broken brown fringes
 in corn fields.

Her clay fingers melting in my tears.

February 1998
Published in *At the Edgelessness of Light,*
James McGrath, Sunstone Press, 2005.

One day

One day
       I shall be a cloud
       and I shall bring you the storm
       who is enrgy
         and song
         and dance
         and growth
         and creativity.

       I shall cross the sky
         and I shall cross the earth.
         I shall pause with you.

I shall sing and dance and grow forever
         and in that myth
         I shall return
         again and again
         to earth
         to myself
         and continue in the myth
         that is the gray fox
         that is the yellow fox
            and that is the sun
            and that is love.

1973
Hotevilla, the Hopi Reservation, Arizona. From *Loloma*,
by James McGrath, American Indian Art Series, KAET/PBS

Otellie's Poem

Star People, gleaming.

Crystals of the sky.

Diamonds of the sky.

      As they formed a circle
      To dance.
      As they danced
      As their songs
      Their bells

Were heard throughout the

Sky spirits world.

      As they dance
      To the rhythms of the
      Earth Mother as it

Moves on.

Listening to their songs

Listening to their bells

As they circle the sky

Let us dance and dance

With the Star people.

Otellie Loloma, Sipaulovi, Second Mesa, Arizona

 90

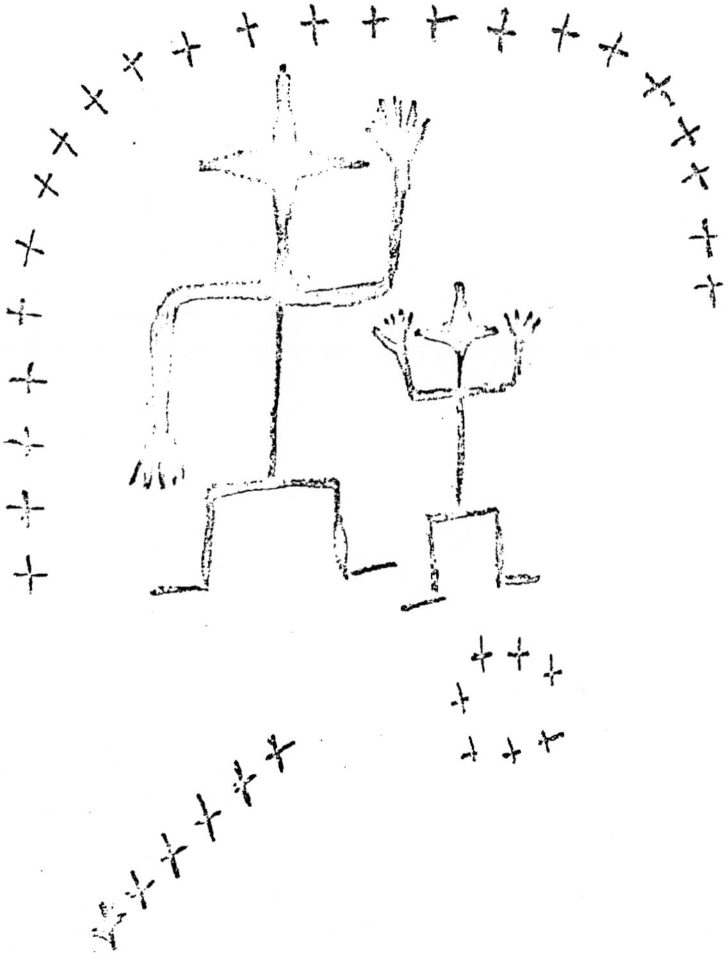

 *About the Artist: Otellie Loloma*

*I*n 1991, Otellie received the Honor Award from the National Women's Center for Arts in Washington DC with the following comment:

> *Otellie Loloma, we honor you for your dedication to what is creative, beautiful and eternal in your Hopi Indian culture. You are honored for your ancient tradition of creating new forms of art from the traditions of your Hopi people. You have made Hopi visible for all of us to share through your arts.*

Petroglyphs of Otellie's Sun Clan are carved throughout the Southwest United States. She was born, raised and educated in her home village, Sipaulovi, went to school at the Bureau of Indian Affairs school on the Hopi Reservation, married Charles Loloma, renowned Hopi jeweler, and taught—until retiring in 1988—at the Institute of American Indian Arts in Santa Fe, New Mexico.

In the Hopi way, she was named *Sequafnehma*, The-place-in-the-valley-where-the-squash-blossoms-bloom. She baked bread and made *pikami* and *piki* with her mother and aunts and went to the old village peach orchard with her grandmother and to the cornfields with her Uncle Ned. As a child she made clay doll sculptures and wrapped them in small cradleboards made of sticks.

Her artwork was exhibited and featured in the Women of Sweetgrass Cedar and Sage Tour, in the Center for Arts of Indian America in Washington DC, in the Museo de Bellas Artes in Buenos Aires, the Biblioteca Nacionale in Santiago, Chile, the Edinburgh and Berlin Festivals, and in England, Mexico and Turkey. She received an award at the Philbrook Annual American Indian Exhibition at the Scottsdale National Indian Arts Exhibition in Arizona.

She danced in the traditional groups at the 1968 Mexican Olympics and in a special invitational program at the White House in 1966.

Otellie said of her work: "Most of my ideas come from the stories told to me at home by uncles, my father and neighbors when I was growing up at Hopi. Winter at Hopi is cold and we stay inside a lot. This is storytelling time. These are the stories of Soyoko, the Kachinas and Yaya times. These stories are of Hopi men and women, animals and birds and Spider Woman. Many of my paintings, drawings, clay figures and portraits on my pots are real characters at Hopi. Some of them are from my imagination and feelings about how I think they might look. Many are dressed in traditional Hopi fashion and are memories of early days. I want to show how things were before. When I work with figures in clay or other media, I think of them as a part of my life and visualize them as I work."

Otellie created the drawings in this book with the poet James McGrath as if traveling on the same path with him. While the poet described his visions of the adventurer as the hunter and the hunted, she brought her visual images and his word images to life and gave expression to the spirit world of the poet.

—James McGrath, 2013

About the Poet: James McGrath

Born in 1928 in Tacomo, Washington, James McGrath lived childhood summers with Napoleon Bernier, his Chehalis Indian uncle, and his Aunt Sinnie on the Nuwaukum River. James is a wanderer about the earth, frequently straying about Greece, Japan, Ireland, Yemen, and the mythically related lands of Hopi and the Pueblos of New Mexico and Arizona.

He is known for his narrative poetry in the KAET/PBS American Indian Artist Series of the 1970s: *Charles Loloma, Allan Houser, R. C. Gorman, Lonewolf and Morning Flower, Helen Hardin* and *Fritz Scholder*. His poems have been published in over twenty anthologies, and his four collections were published by Sunstone Press of Santa Fe, New Mexico.

James was Creative Writing, Painting and Design Training Instructor and Director of Art in the 1960s and 1970s and was Dean of the College in 1988-89 and 1990 at the Institute of American Indian Arts in Santa Fe.

He spent twenty years as Teacher and as Arts and Humanities Coordinator for the US Department of Defense Overseas Schools in Europe and the Far East.

He was poet-artist-in-residence with the US Information Service, Arts America in Yemen, Saudi Arabia, and in the Republic of the Congo in the 1990s.

James was designer and escort officer for the US State Department, Department of the Interior, first International Exhibition of Native American Arts at the Edinburgh Festival, 1966; the Horniman Museum, London, 1966; the Berlin Festival, 1966; the Turkish American Center, Ankara, 1967; the Biblioteca Nacionale, Santiago, Chile, 1967; the Museo de Bellas Artes, Buenos Aires, 1967; the 1968 Mexican Olympics, and the Alaskan Centennial in Anchorage in 1969.

In 2008 he was designated a Santa Fe Living Treasure and in 2012 was given the Gratitude Award by the New Mexico Literary Arts for his contribution to the literary life of New Mexico.

James regularly attends the Listowel Writers' Week in Listowel, County Kerry, Ireland, and has worked with Natalie Goldberg, Joan Logghe, Sharon Olds, David Whyte, Mark Doty, Marjorie Agosin, Alastair Reid, Nuala Ni Dhomhnaill, and Eilis Ni Dhuibhne.

He says of this book: "This poem, these songs became a living part of my adventures while living in New Mexico and Arizona among the Native American people, particularly the Hopi and the Pueblos.

"The seeds of the songs were born during a hunting trip with Santo Domingo Pueblo friends. The rhythm, the music, grew and chorused through the many years spent visiting, eaching and sharing at Hotevilla, Hopi Reservation.

"My deep friendship with Otellie Laloma was the catalyst for creating this book—our gift to one another and our gift to you. This is our harvest."

Santa Fe photographer, Laura Gilpin, photographed James
McGrath and Otellie Loloma in the foothills of the Sangre de Cristo
Mountains outside Santa Fe for the catalog, *Three from Santa Fe*
(with Fritz Scholder). The exhibition was held at the
Center for the Arts of the American Indian in
Washington DC, May 6 through June 28, 1968.

CPSIA information can be obtained
at www.ICGtesting.com
Printed in the USA
FSOW01n1747150817
37458FS